THE WAY OF THE CROSS

HANS-URS VON BALTHASAR

THE WAY
OF THE CROSS

Illustrations by C. Oswald (XIX century)

St. Paul Books & Media

Original Title: *Kreuzweg*
First published as *Via Crucis*
Copyright 1988 Libreria Editrice Vaticana, Città del Vaticano
Illustrations: Copyright Biblioteca Apostolica Vaticana

Translated from German by John G. Cumming

St. Paul Publications
Middlegreen, Slough SL3 6BT, England

Printed and published in the U.S.A. by St. Paul Books & Media

St. Paul Books & Media is the publishing house of the Daughters of
St. Paul, an international congregation of women religious serving the
Church with the communications media.

Introductory prayer of the Holy Father

Lord Jesus Christ,
everyday we receive in the holy Eucharist
the Body and Blood which you left us
as a memorial of your passion
and death on the cross.
Often we do not consider how much this
great gift to your Church had cost you.
You accept us with the same love
with which you embraced the cross.
Give us now the courage to reverently follow
in your footsteps so that we may come to share
in the fruits of your redemption.

Mary's journey of faith even to the Cross

At the foot of the cross Mary, perfectly united with Christ, shares in the shocking mystery of his self-emptying. This is perhaps the deepest "kenosis" of faith in human history.

Through faith the Mother shares in the redeeming death of her Son; but in contrast with the faith of the disciples who fled, hers was far more enlightened.

On Golgotha, Jesus through the cross definitively confirmed that he was the "sign of contradiction" foretold by Simeon. At the same time, there were also fulfilled on Golgotha the words which Simeon had addressed to Mary: "and a sword will pierce through your own soul also".

This new maternity of Mary, generated by faith, is the fruit of the "new" love which came to definitive maturity in her at the foot of the cross, through her sharing in the redemptive love of her Son.

From the Encyclical Letter *Redemptoris Mater* 18.23

Opening prayer

In the name of the Father, and of the Son
and of the Holy Spirit.

R/. Amen

The way of the cross of Jesus
is the regal way of the Church.
Following closely in the footsteps of the Master,
she makes her pilgrimage of faith
to reach the glory of the resurrection.
Let us pray for the gift of the Spirit
so that we may contemplate
Christ's glorious passion
with the loyalty and love
with which Mary followed Jesus
all the way to Calvary.

Pause

Holy and merciful Father,
grant that we may follow the way of the cross
in faith and love, so that we may share
in Christ's passion and together with him
reach the glory of your kingdom.
We ask you this through your Son Jesus Christ.

R/. Amen.

I

Jesus
is condemned
to death

JESUS IS CONDEMNED TO DEATH

V/. We adore you, O Christ, and we bless you.
R/. Because by your holy cross you have redeemed the world.

"So Pilate, wishing to satisfy the crowd, released for them Barabbas; and having scourged Jesus, he delivered him to be crucified." (Mk 15:15)

✠

"He came to his own home, and his own people received him not." The whole world – a world made up of Christians, Jews and non-believers – judges its own Creator and Redeemer. It was a judgement passed on Jesus by a small group among those who had followed him: by Judas who, not finding this Messiah up to his expectations, betrayed him to the Jews who were seeking political power and liberation. Peter denied Jesus, while the other disciples fled.

This is the plain truth about the fledgling Church in moments of trial. Even the Jews did not find in Jesus the ideal figure of the Messiah they dreamt of: a figure so far removed from the faith of Abraham. When they told Pilate that their only king was the emperor, they gave themselves away. Pilate, a pagan, unsuccessfully tried to release Jesus. He gave in to them for the sake of peace in Jerusalem.

No one wanted to admit guilt: Judas rejected the reward of his betrayal; the Jews saw Jesus as a blasphemer who was justly condemned; Pilate washed his hands as a false claim to his innocence. Everybody was guilty but no one wanted to admit it, or to recognize God as he really is.

"For God has consigned all men to disobedience, that

he may have mercy upon all" (Rm 11:32): Christians, Jews and pagans.

Lord our God, have mercy on us all who have condemned you to death. Your mercy is already manifest in the sublime freedom with which you have borne our ingratitude and rejection.

ALL:

Our Father, who art in heaven,
hallowed be thy name;
Thy kingdom come;
Thy will be done on earth as it is in heaven.
Give us this day our daily bread;
and forgive us our trespasses
as we forgive those who trespass against us;
and lead us not into temptation,
but deliver us from evil.

At the cross her station keeping
Stood the mournful Mother weeping,
Close to Jesus to the last.

II

Jesus
takes up
his cross

JESUS TAKES UP HIS CROSS

V/. We adore you, O Christ, and we bless you.
R/. Because by your holy cross you have redeemed the world.

"... Jesus went out, bearing his cross,
to the place called 'Place of the Skull',
which is called in Hebrew Golgotha." (Jn 19:17)

✠

Lord, you accept from humankind the same cross of which from all eternity you told your heavenly Father you were ready to bear in freedom and in love. It was not the human race who placed their sins on your shoulders, making of you a scapegoat, but it was you who had freely taken upon yourself our sins: everything you suffered would have otherwise been in vain. To impose the burden of one's guilt on another is to disclaim any sort of personal culpability. It was not your Father who placed the burden on your shoulders, but the whole Trinity decreed that you should redeem the world lost in sin. You offered yourself to the Father in the Holy Spirit, in order to bring to completion on the cross the work of creation, and the Father – moved by the same Spirit – accepted your sacrifice.

No one would ever conceive that God the Father could send his only Son to the cross in order to restore justice between heaven and earth. All this is the gratuitous work of love. John the Evangelist says expressly that Jesus carried the cross of his own accord (cf. Jn 19:17). Jesus' life was continuously orientated towards the supreme sacrifice. It would all have been useless otherwise. His preaching and miracles failed to convert the people and their leaders, but only made them reject him all the more.

In the end they disowned him precisely on account of his miracles (cf. Jn 11:47-48). He foresaw this: "I have a baptism to be baptized with; and how I am constrained until it is accomplished!" (Lk 12:50).

Welcome, beloved Cross! You are the means by which we can finally and effectively show the world the immensity of God's love.

ALL:

Our Father...

Through her heart, his sorrow sharing,
All his bitter anguish bearing,
Now at length the sword had passed.

III

Jesus
falls for
the first time

JESUS FALLS FOR THE FIRST TIME

V/. We adore you, O Christ, and we bless you.
R/. Because by your holy cross you have redeemed the world.

"Unless a grain of wheat falls into the earth and dies, it remains alone; but if it dies it bears much fruit." (Jn 12:24)

✠

The Bible mentions neither this fall nor the others. But we must remember that Jesus had undergone the appalling Roman scourging, the pain and exhaustion enough to kill anyone.

With repeated blows of the cudgel, the crown of thorns was driven into his sacred head. It is astonishing how our Lord did not lose consciousness when the heavy weight of the cross was placed on his shoulders. His resources were not totally drained.

As long as a human being possesses the inner strength to bear suffering, he is capable of averting the final breakdown. But our Lord was forced to suffer beyond human endurance. We truly understand this when we realize that in his extreme weakness he had to bear not only the burden of the cross but also of our sins – from Adam to the very last person.

We shall never comprehend what this implies because only the Son of God could take upon himself this inconceivable burden. It is quite understandable that such a weight would crush him to the ground. "But I am a worm and not a man," so the Psalmist says of Jesus. We all have a share in it. Each of our sins, which is a rejection of God's love, is like kicking the Lord as he lies exhausted on the ground.

People of goodwill can surely help the Redeemer as he carries his cross. There are those who wish to do so, and we shall encounter them as we go along.

Let us now ask our Lord to forgive us, for we too have placed unnecessary burdens on his shoulders.

ALL:

Our Father...

Oh, how sad and sore distressed
Was that Mother highly blest
Of the sole-begotten one!

IV

Jesus
meets
his mother

JESUS MEETS HIS MOTHER

V/. We adore you, O Christ, and we bless you.
R/. Because by your holy cross you have redeemed the world.

"Simeon said to Mary, "This child is set for the fall and rising of many in Israel, and for a sign that is spoken against and a sword will pierce through your own soul also'." (Lk 2:34-35).

✠

As Mary, the mother, played an essential role in Jesus' conception and birth, likewise she played an essential part in his passion by sharing in his suffering and death. No one is without a companion or a friend, yet on the cross the two criminals crucified with Jesus were of no comfort to him; he needed the presence of the sinless woman, Mary, the ever-Virgin Mother, whom he would make the mother of his mystical body, the Church. To accomplish this, she must be with her son up to the very end of his passion: only from Jesus' exhausted body flow water and blood, the sacraments of the Church, and only from her spiritually-pierced heart does Mary become the mother and prototype of her Son's bride, the Church. Jesus entrusts to his sorrowful Mother his beloved disciple, John, who would be spiritually united with Peter, the representative of ecclesial unity. Thus, Mary the Immaculate becomes the Mother of the Petrine Church where – on behalf of all believers – she pleads the Holy Spirit by whom she was overshadowed at Nazareth.

Mary is an ordinary human being, not a quasi-divine creature who could bear the sins of the world. Nonetheless she has a part to play in this suffering that is beyond all human reckoning: she is asked not to rebel against it,

but to accept it to the bitter end. Such a sacrifice cannot be asked of any one nor of any woman nor of any mother. The symbol of the seven swords piercing her heart is only a faint indication of what she suffered, as the author of Revelation says: "a great portent in heaven: a woman with child crying out in her pangs of birth, in anguish for delivery " (Rev 12:1-2). We are partly indebted to Mary for our being Christians – a gift coming totally from God. The Fathers of the Church were in fact aware that Christians have God for Father and the Marian Church for Mother. On the way to Calvary Mary could not fully take upon herself the sufferings of her Son but she could only say "yes" walking alongside with him. This is the Christian calling: having embraced the cross Christ invites us to carry it with him, enabling us to share in the fruits of the redemption.

Mary, our Virgin Mother, on the way to Calvary,
you met Jesus carrying his cross. His face showed
anguish, and his limbs were weak with pain.
He did not complain, and his eyes were full of love.
You met him and you understood.
With him you climbed the hill of sacrifice,
and you shared in his suffering for our salvation.
Teach us, Virgin Mother, to recognize your Son
in the oppressed, the outcast and the despised.
Show us to walk by his side until his face shines
with hope and, in the light of the cross,
his agony is changed into joy.

ALL:

Our Father...

Christ above in torment hangs,
She beneath beholds the pangs
of her dying glorious Son.

V

Simon of Cyrene
helps Jesus
carry his cross

SIMON OF CYRENE HELPS JESUS CARRY HIS CROSS

V/. We adore you, O Christ, and we bless you.
R/. Because by your holy cross you have redeemed the world.

"And they compelled a passerby, Simon of Cyrene, who was coming in from the country, the father of Alexander and Rufus, to carry his cross." (Mk 15:21)

✠

Mary, in the most profound sorrow, accompanies her son on his way to Calvary. Simon, an ordinary man, is not prepared for anything unusual. He is on his way home from work. The evangelists underline the fact that he had to be forced to carry the cross that is too heavy for Jesus.

How many of us are unexpectedly burdened with a load that we cannot shake off: sickness, death in the family or, worse still, exile, eviction, to have one's property confiscated, or famine. Whether we like it or not we have to suffer one way or another. It is useless to kick the goad because suffering is part of being human: its acceptance ennobles the spirit, thus uniting us to Jesus and to all those who suffer. Even our most feeble "yes" to suffering – despite our resistance and our being unaware of it – becomes a transforming grace, provided that we accept it from the hands of God. Job, a patient man, uttered bitter words for his undeserved fate and great suffering, nevertheless was able to accept everything as coming from God: "The Lord has given and the Lord has taken away. The Lord's name be praised," – this earned him God's justification.

What then are we to do? We should not rebel against

God and what he planned for us, but strive to do God's will in all things. Suffering is a sign that God wants us to be associated with his Son's work of redemption. We must have the courage to take up our cross daily and un-grudgingly, knowing that the Lord bore much more than we could possibly think of.

ALL:

Our Father…

Is there anyone who would not weep,
Whelmed in miseries so deep,
Christ's dear Mother to behold?

VI

Veronica
wipes the face
of Jesus

VERONICA WIPES THE FACE OF JESUS

V/. We adore you, O Christ, and we bless you.
R/. Because by your holy cross you have redeemed the world.

"He had no form or comeliness that we should look at him, and no beauty to attract us. He was despised and rejected by men as one from whom men hide their faces." (Is 53:2-3)

☩

Veronica is not mentioned in the Bible, but several women were present along the way to Calvary: women who wished by their presence, not only to profess their faith in the Lord but also to help him unreservedly.

Women in the Gospel are marked by Christ's preferential love of which John, the beloved disciple, was privileged. The Church, the bride of Christ, is therefore graced by the presence of women. In so far as the Church professes her faith and fidelity in loving humility to the Lord, as Veronica did in a gesture of love, Jesus leaves the imprint of his features on all those who are ready to accept it as a peace-token of his love.

The Christian who bears the image of Christ in his heart, will recognize the same features of Christ in his suffering brothers and sisters. "What you do to the least of my brethren, you do it to me." Everyone can offer help to the suffering, be it only a glass of water or, in the impossibility of giving material help, an open heart ready to sustain them in moments of loneliness and despair.

Faced with the inevitable sufferings in the world, which are daily portrayed by the media, we all feel our inability

to cope, like the disciples who, before a great multitude to feed, wondered "*what five loaves and two fish are for so many*".

We can always pray the Lord who has the power to work the miracle of the multiplication of loaves and fish, and alleviate the sufferings of many.

Veronica's linen cloth, bearing the features of Jesus, is a sign and a promise to all believers that he will help them who call upon him.

Lord God, imprint in my spirit the sufferings of your Son Jesus.

ALL:

Our Father...

Can the human heart refrain
From partaking in her pain,
In that Mother's pain untold?

VII

Jesus
falls for the
second time

JESUS FALLS FOR THE SECOND TIME

V/. We adore you, O Christ, and we bless you.
R/. Because by your holy cross you have redeemed the world.

*"Jesus said to them, 'My soul is very sorrowful, even to death…"
And going a little farther, he fell on the ground and prayed that,
if it were possible, this hour might pass from him." (Mk 14:34-35)*

✠

To know that the Son of God's strength should fail him is indeed terrifying, yet it reminds us of what John (3:16) says of him: "God so loved the world that he gave his only Son…" to take upon himself the weight of man's sins and, as man, succumb under it. Humanly speaking, what would the Father have felt upon seeing his Son's sufferings, who in fulfilment of his Father's will gave himself up to death?

No words are able to describe the "compassion" of the Father towards his Son who had to undergo such intense pain for love of sinful man. In his *Spiritual Exercises* St Ignatius says that we should reflect on "God's passion and care for us like someone engaged in an arduous task" (n. 236). The Son of God, unlike the mythical Atlas, bears the world upon his shoulders out of love, and is crushed to the ground under its heavy weight.

We always want to know why God allows so much suffering in the world. There is no easy answer to this. God can only offer a gesture of fatherly love: he loves the world so much that "he gave his only Son" to fall and be crushed under its massive weight. God's infinite love for fallen man is the same as that of his Son, whose love for

us was so great that he took our guilt upon himself in order to restore our relationship with the Father. The Holy Spirit is the bond of love between the Father and Son, and we, in the Spirit, are encompassed in the same love.

We should not dwell so much on our own suffering which is nothing compared to what the Son of God suffered for us. Whenever we are able to share in a small way in Christ's suffering, it is indeed a grace.

ALL:

Our Father

Bruised, derided, cursed, defiled
She beheld her tender Child
All with bloody scourges rent.

VIII

Jesus
comforts the
women of Jerusalem

JESUS COMFORTS THE WOMEN OF JERUSALEM

V/. We adore you, O Christ, and we bless you.
R/. Because by your holy cross you have redeemed the world.

"And there followed him a great multitude of the people, and of women who bewailed and lamented him. But Jesus turning to them said, 'Daughters of Jerusalem, do not weep for me, but weep for yourselves and for your children'." (Lk 23:27-28)

✠

In this station we are faced with a gnawing question about the role played by the people of Israel in the Passion of Jesus.

We cannot ignore the fact that Israel not only disowned its long-awaited Messiah, but also condemned him to death; we should nonetheless bear in mind that both pagans and Christians are also guilty of his death. Jesus however would not let himself be comforted by the women of Jerusalem: "…weep not for me but for yourselves and for your children". He foresees the imminent catastrophe which is to befall Jerusalem, and indeed the whole of Israel. He sees the oncoming rift which tears of compassion cannot avert. "How often would I have gathered your children together… and you would not!" (Lk 13:34). The people of Israel could not give solace to the Son of God while he is being condemned.

We are faced here with a dilemma concerning God's plan so much so that even St Paul, after having tried to understand more deeply the relation between Israel and the gentiles, exclaims: "How unsearchable are his judge-

ments and how inscrutable his ways!" (Rm 11:33). Who would ever understand that the harsh fate that has fallen upon the people of Israel would redound to the benefit of us Christians who came from the Gentiles? We must realize therefore that if we have been graced by God through Israel's misfortune, we owe them respect and gratitude as to our elder brothers and sisters. How could we abandon them knowing that God's promises to Israel are irrevocable?

O Mary our mother,
you too wept and lamented
on Calvary with the women
of Jerusalem.

You weep not for yourself,
because, in faith and in obedience,
you did the Father's will;
nor did you lament over
the death of your Son,
the innocent and holy One.

You weep instead for the sins
of your children.
We have seen your tears,
heard your warnings and entreaties:
"do not suppress truth,
do not persecute the innocent,
do not smother love".

ALL:

Our Father...

Let me share with you his pain
who for all my sins was slain
who for me in torment died.

IX

Jesus
falls for the
third time

JESUS FALLS FOR THE THIRD TIME

V/. We adore you, O Christ, and we bless you.
R/. Because by your holy cross you have redeemed the world.

"Come to me, all who labour and are heavy-laden, and I will give you rest. Take my yoke upon you, and learn from me; for I am gentle and lowly in heart, and you will find rest for your souls. For my yoke is easy, and my burden is light." (Mt 11:28-30)

✠

It would not be inappropriate to think that this third fall of Jesus came about to the advantage of the people of Israel. Jesus' greatest pain was possibly the rejection by his own people who condemned him to the most atrocious death. We should not forget that his first mission was to gather together the scattered sheep of Israel. He came primarily – as he openly declared and was fully aware of – as the last of the many messengers sent by God to the House of Israel. Not having been recognized as the Messiah was the most poignant defeat and the greatest humiliation he had to undergo.

This last burden, surely, must redound to Israel's advantage: how could it be otherwise? The tears of the daughters of Jerusalem could undoubtedly mingle with the tears of Jesus over that city whose destruction was imminent (cf. Lk 19:41).

In the end, according to St Paul "all Israel will be saved" (Rm 11:26), and who else but Israel's Messiah, who has become the Saviour of the entire human race, could bring this about?

Christ has encompassed in his passion the sufferings of the people of Israel. This could be taken as a prelude

to the salvation spoken of by Luke in his account of Jesus' death: that all those who had witnessed it went home beating their breasts (cf. Lk 23:48).

ALL:

Our Father...

O my Mother, fount of love,
Touch my spirit from above;
Make my heart with yours accord.

X

Jesus
is stripped
of his garments

JESUS IS STRIPPED OF HIS GARMENTS

V/. We adore you, O Christ, and we bless you.
R/. Because by your holy cross you have redeemed the world.

"They divided his garments among them, casting lots for them, to decide what each should take." (Mk 15:24)

✠

What do clothes matter to a human body which is about to be crucified? Jesus is stripped of his garments to enable the soldiers to work without being hampered.

Since that time in the Garden of Eden, fallen man has been covering himself with all sorts of clothing: from fig leaves and animal skins to the latest fashion of today. On Calvary everything is cast away: the new Adam stands before the Father as he is, having freely taken upon himself the sins and shame of the old Adam. God the Father is presented with naked humanity: what he made, what has turned away from him and what has been brought back to him – all of which is revealed in Jesus' body.

On the cross man fully manifests himself, and God restores to him his lost dignity – his most precious gift to mankind. In every eucharistic celebration down the centuries he gives to humanity this unadorned body. "The body of Christ" – says the priest as he gives communion – "who takes away the sins of the world": the body which bears your sins and the wounds inflicted on it.

The Father sees the old Adam – whom we all represent – being regenerated in Jesus, the new Adam. Mary too, the sorrowful mother, seeing his Son stripped of his gar-

ments, recalls the time when she carried him in her womb and gave birth to him. What she experiences now may be likened to a second birth, nonetheless more fruitful than the first. Mary, together with the Father, gives to humanity the body of Christ who, under the most atrocious suffering, gave himself freely to all.

ALL:

Our Father...

Make me feel as you have felt,
Make my soul to glow and melt
with the love of Christ my Lord.

XI

Jesus
is nailed
to the cross

ELEVENTH STATION

JESUS IS NAILED TO THE CROSS

V/. We adore you, O Christ, and we bless you.
R/. Because by your holy cross you have redeemed the world.

"It was the third hour, when they crucified him. And the inscription of the charge against him read, 'The King of the Jews'. And with him they crucified two robbers, one on his right and one on his left." (Mk 15:25-27)

✠

"They know not what they do" (Lk 23:34). They nailed him to the cross in order to get rid of him, but in so doing, bonded him the more firmly to the earth. They nailed him down so that he could no longer go away but remain with us forever: neither the Resurrection nor the Ascension could alter this.

No one binds Jesus to sinful humanity; he remains with us, of his own accord, to the very end. And when he returns on judgement day the cross, "the sign of the Son of man, will appear in heaven" (Mt 24:30). At the time of creation, when the elements were separated, "vertically and horizontally", the world received an initial impression of this sign which was to become the culminating point of universal history.

"All things were created through him and for him" (Col 1:16-17), that is, for the Son whom the Father allows to be nailed to the cross of the world.

This is the mystery of love which surpasses all human philosophies and religions. To be nailed to the cross is the greatest suffering that could ever be inflicted on a victim, but according to John, it is the highest expression of the love of God made man.

Overwhelmed by this unfathomable mystery we can only kneel in grateful adoration.

ALL:

Our Father...

Holy Mother, pierce me through;
In my heart each wound renew
Of my Saviour crucified.

XII

Jesus
dies on
the cross

JESUS DIES ON THE CROSS

V/. We adore you, O Christ, and we bless you.
R/. Because by your holy cross you have redeemed the world.

"And when the sixth hour had come, there was darkness over the whole land until the ninth hour. And at the ninth hour Jesus cried with a loud voice, 'Eloi, Eloi, lama sabachtani?' which means, 'My God, my God, why hast thou forsaken me?' ...And one ran and, filling a sponge full of vinegar, put it on a reed and gave it to him to drink... And Jesus uttered a loud cry, and breathed his last. ...And when the centurion, who stood facing him, saw that he thus breathed his last, he said, 'Truly this man was the Son of God'." (Mk 15:33-39)

✠

Jesus is suspended between heaven and earth, repudiated by men and forsaken by his Father, thus restoring the unity between them. Extending his arms he reaches out to both the sinner who goes back to him and to the one who turns away from him and yet could not hinder Christ to reach out to him. The vertical beam of the cross bridges the gap between God and man, while the horizontal one embraces the ends of the earth. The Fathers of the Church therefore could aptly say that the Cross had the dimensions of the whole creation; it has the dimensions of the whole history of the human race because in these three long hours of Christ's agony, the sins of all – from the first person to the very last – have been gathered and remitted. From now on the way to heaven is open to all: this is the teaching of the Church.

The last words of the dying Jesus express his entire testament to the Church: that the Father will surely, indeed he must, forgive us, wretched and ignorant as we

are; that Easter will be the great absolution, setting the seal on our final reconciliation with God; and that the sinless Mother is placed at the centre of the Church which, despite the sinfulness of its members, preserves its core intact.

Jesus' forsaken death on the cross opened for us the way to the Father. The thirst of Christ's body, drained of every drop of blood, makes of it a spring from whence flow waters of eternal life. Both the water of baptism and the blood of the Eucharist quench our thirst. In the dying cry of Jesus God reveals to us his infinite love which transcends the power of words.

Bending his head, Jesus gives up the Spirit, the same Spirit whom he will breathe on the Church on the day of his Resurrection, and in this way all is truly accomplished.

Holy Mary, Virgin of the cross:
by the tree of life, you are humanity itself:
obedient and faithful, receptive to the word,
resolute and dutiful, open to the Spirit.

Reveal to us the mystery of the "Hour" of your Son:
of his glory in disgrace,
of his majesty in service,
of our life in his death.

But it is also your "Hour", O Virgin Mary:
the hour of birth – in faith, in pain, in the Spirit;
for that new birth, Jesus, dying on the cross,
said: "Woman, behold your son."

ALL:

Our Father…

For the sins of his own nation
She saw him hang in desolation
Till his spirit forth he sent.

XIII

Jesus
is taken down
from the cross

THIRTEENTH STATION

JESUS IS TAKEN DOWN FROM THE CROSS

V/. We adore you, O Christ, and we bless you.
R/. Because by your holy cross you have redeemed the world.

"Standing by the cross of Jesus were his mother, and her mother's sister, Mary the wife of Clopas, and Mary Magdalene... The soldiers came to Jesus and when they saw that he was already dead, they did not break his legs. But one of the soldiers pierced his side with a spear, and at once there came out blood and water. After this Joseph of Arimathea... asked Pilate that he might take away the body of Jesus." (Jn 19:25.32-24.38)

✠

Jesus is taken down from the cross and his mother – accepting the pain that his Son bore for the sake of the world – is there to receive him in her bosom. Each of the seven swords which transfixed the heart of the mother was Mary's renewed assent to her Son's sufferings. It is beyond human comprehension that a person should say "yes" to everything, even to the most harrowing pain.

In her unconditional "yes" Mary becomes the "redeemed earth", capable of receiving on her lap the dead body of the Redeemer. This scene wrapped in silence reveals that Christ's Passion was not suffered in vain: Mary in this moment of weariness and infinite sorrow, represents humanity who accepts with gratitude heaven's blessings. In the end her Son's body is not buried in a cold and inanimate matter ("matter" comes from the Latin word *mater* meaning "mother") but it is placed in the maternal and fruitful bosom of Mary, a prototype of incarnate love which finds its culmination in Mary. The *Pietà* therefore

is not a fleeting image of sorrow but one engraved forever
in human history: a mysterious image portraying maternal
fecundity enshrouding the dead Son's body – the source
of a new fecundity for the mother.

Holy Mary,
in your virginal bosom,
lies your dead Son;
you are the living *pietà*,
who maternally embrace
all your lost children,
the wounded, and the dead.

Teach us, O Mary,
how to show true compassion,
a compassion nourished
by love alone;
that immense compassion
which knows no bounds;
active compassion which –
gazing on human suffering –
raises suppliant eyes to heaven.

ALL:

Our Father...

Let me mingle tears with you
Mourning him who mourned for me,
All the days that I may live.

XIV

Jesus
is laid
in the tomb

JESUS IS LAID IN THE TOMB

V/. We adore you, O Christ, and we bless you.
R/. Because by your holy cross you have redeemed the world.

"When Pilate learned from the centurion that Jesus was dead, he granted the body to Joseph. And he bought a linen shroud, and taking him down, wrapped him in the linen shroud, and laid him in a tomb which had been hewn out of the rock; and he rolled a stone against the entrance of the tomb. Mary Magdalene and Mary the mother of Joses saw where he was laid."
(Mk 15:45-47)

✠

The fact that Jesus' body – wrapped in a linen shroud – lay in the tomb for three days, rules out any possibility of apparent death. He died as all people die. A large stone indicates definitiveness: everything that had been lived until then is now decisively in the past.

Nevertheless Jesus' death – a death which is absolutely real – was different from any other. For this unique death was the ultimate expression of God's infinite love, and love is the only living reality that cannot die. Precisely when love decides to die for the sake of another, it can show that it is capable of transforming even death into a sign and instrument of life. It should not be difficult for a Christian to understand this.

Love is nothing else but perfect self-oblation and ab-negation, in order to give oneself completely to the loved one. Is this not a form of death? And when one loves in a Christian way, placing his life completely at the service of his neighbour, is this not a "dying to self"?

When we say with St John that God is love (1 Jn 4:8), is this not an oblative "dying to self" in the life of the

Trinity? God is Father because he gives himself totally to the Son, and this is also true of the Son and of the Holy Spirit. A Christian therefore who abandons himself wholly to God and his dying Son, can turn his "dying-to-self" into a life-giving love.

Jesus dies and is buried: even St Paul points this out unequivocally (1 Cor 15:4); but since Jesus' death was a life-giving death, the tomb could not retain him: "Christ has been raised from the dead, the first fruits of those who have fallen asleep. For as in Adam all men die, so also in Christ shall all be made alive" (1 Cor 15:20-22).

ALL:

Our Father...

While my body here decays,
May my soul your goodness praise,
Safe in paradise with you. Amen.

"He descended to the dead.
On the third day he rose again.
He ascended into heaven,
and is seated at the right hand of the Father..."

From the Apostles' Creed